Inspirational Poems

by

Divine Purpose

The Poetry and Artwork of

June Haines

Copyright page

But God: Inspirational Poems
Author June Haines
Artist and Illustrator: June Haines

www.fordivinepurpose.com
info@fordivinepurpose.com

Published by Olmstead Publishing
1631 Rock Springs Rd, Apopka, FL 32712-2229;
407-814-8770.
ISBN: 978-1-934194-18-8

September 2007

FORWARD

My Dear Friend and Sister in Christ, Mighty Woman of God,

I am so excited, humbled, honored, and truly proud of this anointed work and you! It has only been three years since your spiritual re-birthday, and God, through the Holy Spirit, has moved and "birthed" a powerful and wonderful work .... messages for His people, through you.

In one's life there are many variations of choices, consequently decisions are factors of the outcome of our fate. BUT GOD!

In life, the greatest choice of all is deciding to follow Jesus; resulting in a fate of grace, unconditional love and prosperity to expand beyond our lives into our children's and children's children's lives and beyond, according to our Father's promise.

I thank God for placing it upon your heart to reach out to the world, through the expressions in your poems. My prayer is that every reader of this book will be as blessed while reading it, as you were while writing it.

Love from your sister,

Jacqueline Shaw Johnson

Divine Purpose Ministries

Table of Contents

Peace Be Still 6
Only You 7
Thank You Lord 8
Standing On His Promise 10
Glory of the Lord 12
Holding On 14
God Delivered Me 16
He Has Already Provided 17
Do You Know 19
Always Something New 21
Lord I Need You 22
Sit Back 24
My Life 25
His Grace is Sufficient 26
This is the Day 27
It is Time 29
Touch Not My Anointed and Do My Prophet No Harm 30
Satan is Defeated 32
Get Right 33
Tithes 34
Waiting for My Boaz 35
Author Biography 36

When you are going through a storm, call on Jesus and He will say,

"Peace Be Still..."

he arose, and rebuked the wind, and said unto the sea, Peace, be still. And the wind ceased, and there was a great calm.   Mark 4 : 39

ONLY YOU

I am tired, and weak, I need some strength, casting down all things that have me bound, pick me up, turn me around, place my feet on solid ground.

Only You, can do what You do, Awesome Lord, I believe You. Cast all your cares on Him because He cares for you, put all your trust in Him is what He said to do. Making things happen when we just trust You.

In my time of need I will call on Him, and He will answer me. Saying I am here and always near, no fear, no doubt, just rejoice and shout!

Praising the Lord all day long, I will find a place in my heart, to keep a special song.

Casting all your care upon him; for he careth for you. 1 Peter 5 : 7

THANK YOU LORD

I thank you and I love you for everything you've done, with you in my life there has been so much that I've overcome. All the people in my life can never compare, to Jesus Christ who's always been there.

Hanging on the corner or staying in the streets, what good are we to anyone if we can't get on our feet? Can you stand on your own with no one around, and keep your head up and your feet on the ground.

We seem to think that we can do it all by ourselves, but in reality we all need help.

Even as a soldier I still get weak, I have to call on the Lord to get more strength.

I tell Him, "Lord I can not make it by myself; right now I need you to put me on a shelf."

Only for a season, no one knowing the reason, how you make me made me; shape me, form me into your image, being more like Christ. Wanting to walk in the abundant life, of all that He has just for me liberty, victory, and prosperity.

I just want to say thank you Lord for the power of Faith and the strength to win this race.

Giving thanks always for all things unto God and the Father in the name of our Lord Jesus Christ;
Ephesians 5 : 20

STANDING ON HIS PROMISE

I am standing on the promises of God everyday; wanting Him to use me, in a special way. Going thru these tests, trials, and pain; calling on you Lord and not in vain. I need you in my life all the time keeping you close so I remain the same with a heart sold out for you. Lord, I worship you and I praise you. I have come to realize that I am nothing without you.

I am standing on His promises and waiting for the day; that He will use me in a special way. Glory to your name and everything you are because of your Grace and Mercy you've made me what I am this far.

We all have choices that we make everyday we can serve you Lord or we can go astray. Quitting is not an option for me I will fight this fight and walk this walk until the end. Again I say I am standing on your promises and waiting for the day, that you will use me Lord in a special way.

So many days and so many nights going thru this battle sometimes I become too tired to fight. So I find myself in a quiet place on my knees I will seek your face. I am standing on your promises and waiting for the day, that you will use me Lord in a special way.

Watch ye, stand fast in the faith, quit you like men, be strong.
I Corinthians 16 : 13

GLORY OF THE LORD

Let the glory of Lord and the promise of His word; manifest it self in you like never before.

He is a god that can not lie; His promise is the same 'til you die.

When times get rough, and when you try to be tough, stand back and let the glory of the Lord and the promise of His word, rise up in you and shine thru you like never before.

But we all, with open face beholding as in a glass the glory of the Lord, are changed into the same image from glory to glory, even as by the Spirit of the Lord.
2 Corinthians 3 : 18

The Glory of the Lord over the earth...

HOLDING ON

Can you stand the rain, without going insane, enduring the pain on a constant chain? Begging the Lord to pull you out, of all this mess, all you can do is shout.

Help me! Is all I can say, the joy of the Lord is my strength. We don't know how our pain and sorrows will end, but if we just trust in God He will mend, every broken heart and wipe way every tear.

Trusting in you Lord, I will not fear the power of man and knowing that you are near.

I can do all thru Christ, who strengthens me. Thank you, Lord, for the VICTORY.

*Then he said unto them, Go your way, eat the fat, and drink the sweet, and send portions unto them for whom nothing is prepared: for this day is holy unto our LORD: neither be ye sorry; for **the joy of the LORD** is your strength.* Nehemiah 8 : 10

His master replied, 'Well done, good and faithful servant! You have been faithful with a few things; I will put you in charge of many things. Come and share your master's happiness!' Matthew 25 : 21,23

But
GOD

GOD DELIVERED ME

Thank you Lord for delivering me from that miserable life of poverty.

Dancing all night trying to be cute acting like I was in a 2 Live Crew shoot.

Men all around every corner I went, only made me want to be a little pimp. I couldn't decide which one I wanted so I picked a few and I flaunted and used them any way I could. Always drinkin' and smokin' whatever I could, caught up in the streets and up to no good.

So many nights I was too drunk to drive, and still got behind the wheel not caring if I survived. God only knows why I arrived alive.

All of the negative attention I was trying to get almost sent me to the fiery pit. The pit of Hell is what it's called, but it's the price you pay when you want to ball. Is the fast life worth the price you have to pay, make the right choice let God deliver you today?

HE HAS ALREADY PROVIDED

He has already provided; nothing divided, trusting Him is all He needs while He blesses your harvest from all of your seeds.

Just like a farmer who waits for His crop to grow, we wait for the day for our harvest to show. Bigger than ever and more for the eye to see, wait on God is the only way it will be.

God can bless you in so many ways, if you can only wait patiently for that day. Doing His will for an audience of one, makes Him want to bless you even the more when you're done.

The way God can bless you is better than man, so delight yourself in Him and He will show that He can. Stop trying to figure out what direction it will come, just trust, and know that He is the only one.

DO YOU KNOW

Do you know what tomorrow will bring? Maybe a house, car, or ring. No one knows what will tomorrow will be, a day of torment or prosperity. You have to speak it in the air, even though life isn't fare.

There is power in your tongue, I want you to know, open your mouth, and it will show. Where do you want your life be, in abundance or poverty?

Make sure your heart is always right, when you start your day and before you go to bed at night. No one knows what tomorrow will bring; your alarm clock might not ring.

Forget about yesterday for it is gone, forget about tomorrow because tomorrow never comes, get right today is all I have to say. Your eternity is only a breath away.

Ephesians 6:11

Put on the whole armour of God,

Helmet of Salvation,

cloak of humility,

and your hands are ready for war.

ALWAYS SOMETHING NEW

Always something new, it's apart of life we have to go through. New trials, new destiny, always a new test in me. Sickness and disease and a whole past life poverty, didn't keep me down, because I passed a new test and found a life of prosperity.

From rags to riches is what you see, now living a life full of the VICTORY. God does not care who you are, or where you're from, He just wants you to get the job done.

Don't let people discourage you, trust in God and He will see you through. Remember there is always going to be a new test just for you.

I will give a nugget to help you win, and that is when the test comes you just jump in. Your gonna go through no matter what you do; the outcome of the tests depends on you.

Seek His direction on everything you do, then waiting patiently on Him to see you through.

LORD I NEED YOU

I love you and I need you everyday and in everyway. Without you in my life, there would be no words that I can say.

I need you every minute and I need you every hour, without you I would have no power. Without you Lord I could not speak, without you Lord I would be weak.

Thank you Lord for Spirit and your power, filled with the Holy Ghost I stand taller than a tower. Praising your name all of the time, walking in the Spirit, letting my light shine.

So many days, so many nights, so many star lights, so many dark nights.

Lord I know that you see all, hear all and you gave us your.

Holy Spirit to guide us so we don't fall.

We take your love for granted a lot of the time, and forget the price you paid when your life was on the line.

Nailed to a cross beaten and bruised, pushed and cursed--you were wrongfully used.

We complain about the simple things, acting like the world owes us "it's a shame." We need to remember ALL that the Lord has done keeping ourselves humble and know that He is the one.

SIT BACK

Sit back and relax yourself, no need to get upset if you can not help, God just said do what you can; everything else is in His plan.

He will do ALL things better than us , sit back and trust, that no matter what you are going thru, hold on you'll come out a better you.

Pure as gold, so fresh and new, strong as ever because that test didn't destroy you. Now get ready because what you go thru ain't even for you, God knew He could use you.

MY LIFE

In my life there has been so many ups and downs, never walking with a smile because there was always a frown.

I didn't know what it felt like to really be happy; so many times I would get upset to see people laughing.

I understood what it felt like to be used and abused, was never accepted but always rejected. No matter how hard I tried to just fit in, it never failed I was rejected again.

Finally the day has come; I grabbed a hold of the Mighty One. When I think back on my life and everything I went thru, then look at me now. God has made me fresh and new.

For if the casting away of them be the reconciling of the world, what shall the receiving of them be, but life from the dead?
Romans 1: 15

And he said unto me, My grace is sufficient for thee: for my strength is made perfect in weakness. Most gladly therefore will I rather glory in my infirmities, that the power of Christ may rest upon me.
2 Corinthians 12 : 9

HIS GRACE IS SUFFICIENT

His grace is sufficient and His love is real. He died on the cross over 2000 years ago to obey His fathers will.

Death for Him meant life for us and even more abundantly if we would only learn to trust.

No matter what it looks like, no matter how it feels, just keep you're eyes on Jesus and He will show you that He is real.

THIS IS THE DAY

This is the day that the Lord has made, I have chosen to rejoice and be glad in it. Victory is mine no matter if it rains or if the sun shines.

I will bless the Lord for the very breath I receive and understand that without Him there is no me. I will obey you Lord, carry my sword, walk in confidence and stand on your word.

No matter how hard the trials of life become, I will seek ye first the kingdom of god and all His righteousness, and know that in my obedience that you will deliver me from everyone.

But seek ye first the kingdom of God, and his righteousness; and all these things shall be added unto you.
Matthew 6 : 33

IT IS TIME

It is time to get in line, get our lives right so our light will shine.

It takes too much time to be fake. If you think that you are fooling people you're making a mistake.

I have tried again and again to keep my head up and staying away from sin.

I can do all things through Christ who strengthens me and put my trust in God and I will see that through Christ Jesus I have the VICTORY!

It is time to get in line. Get our lives right so our light will shine.

Sow to yourselves in righteousness, reap in mercy; break up your fallow ground: for it is time to seek the LORD, till he come and rain righteousness upon you.
Hosea 10 : 12

TOUCH NOT MY ANOINTED AND DO MY PROPHET NO HARM

Take heed to God's word and obey the Lord. Watch what you say and carry your sword.

If there is a problem with a saint, take it to the Lord and then just wait. Let God be God in every way. Leave it there and just continue to pray.

God can correct things better than us. All we have to do is pray and trust.

The eyes of the Lord are in every place. Just keep your mouth off of people and you will be safe.

*Saying, **Touch not** mine anointed, and do my prophets no harm.*
I Chronicles 16 : 22

SATAN IS DEFEATED

Too many people are trying to be fake, acting like Christians you are making a mistake.

Time and time again we get caught up in sin. When are we going to get tired of letting Satan win?

Satan is defeated this is constantly repeated if we just walk up right in the bright light, Jesus said be still and He will fight.

The battle is not mine the battle is not yours stand on god's promises and He will close those doors.

But he turned, and said unto Peter, Get thee behind me, Satan: thou art an offence unto me: for thou savourest not the things that be of God, but those that be of men.
Matthew 16 : 23

GET RIGHT

Today is the day that you have to get right, if you hold on to sin you won't have light. What is it that you really want; to gain the world and lose your soul or choose Christ and be made whole?

Pick up your cross daily and follow Christ and watch how quick you will walk in the abundant life.

For what is a man profited, if he shall gain the whole world, and lose his own soul? or what shall a man give in exchange for his soul? Matthew 16 : 26

TITHES

How many times have you heard the word, paying your Tithes 10% belongs to the Lord. Trying to compromise on how to pay, read the word and it will say, return it to the Storehouse where you are fed, in the house of God is what it said.

Robbing God is not cool at all, on your face you will fall. Cursed with a curse on your family, and walking in the path of poverty.

Take your Tithes out straight from the top, stop! Anything that you receive is an increase you better believe. Trust God and see, that in your obedience, He will take you to the land of prosperity.

[8] Will a man rob God? Yet ye have robbed me. But ye say, Wherein have we robbed thee? In tithes and offerings.

[10] Bring ye all the tithes into the storehouse, that there may be meat in mine house, and prove me now herewith, saith the LORD of hosts, if I will not open you the windows of heaven, and pour you out a blessing, that there shall not be room enough to receive it.
Malachi 3 : 8,10

WAITING FOR MY BOAZ

These feelings inside, Lord I can not hide. I wait patiently for my Boaz to arrive.

Your word says that it is not good for a man to be alone, so I will trust you Lord because you sit on the throne.

He that findeth a wife finds a good thing and obtains favor with God.

So, Lord, help me to keep my eyes on You and I know that you will see me through.

I want your will to be done in my life, and as I wait on you, prepare me to be a good wife.

And, behold, Boaz came from Bethlehem, and said unto the reapers, The LORD be with you. And they answered him, The LORD bless thee.
Ruth 2 : 4

June Elizabeth Haines

I was born in Lake City, South Carolina in 1971 to Myrtis and Richard Haines.

I was raised in Orlando, Florida and is a lifelong resident. I am the 2nd of 3 children and was blessed to have two brothers, Richard and Robert Haines.

I attended school in the Central Florida area, Hillcrest Elementary, Howard Junior High and Edgewater High School. It truly is a blessing to continue to be a resident of an area that it growing.

My four children Chris (17), Latesha (12), Candace (10) and Daniel (8), have been my everything and encourage me to be my best. I am a mighty women of God and I gave my life to Jesus Christ on January 4, 2004. God has truly blessed us. God gave me a talent to paint, not only did he give me a talent, but he has brought me before many great men of God. I am inspired to paint by the Holy Spirit. My paintings are prophetic and depict inspiration scriptures and have been recognized by many.

I am the "519" Pledge drive Commemorative artist in Sanford, Florida. The Mayor of Sanford, Linda Kuhn was presented with one of my paintings as well as the late Hall of Famer, Jackie Robinson's daughter, Sharon Robinson. My paintings have truly been a success and an inspiration to may lives. They have grown in a direction that the Lord has taken them too.

They are currently displayed on greeting cards, T-shirts, tote bags, ties, vases, canvas and mouse pads. I currently have over 200 pieces of art and I am blessed to be chosen for such an honor and I give all the praise to God. BUT GOD, saved me, molded me, filled me and used me to paint these inspiring paintings and I delight in the testimonies that are given from the people who have purchased them. I am patiently awaiting on the progress that these paintings and their financial fruition will take Divine Purpose Ministries and hope that you too are blessed.

Biblical References Indexed By Page Order

Mark 4:39	6
1 Peter 5:7	7
Ephesians 5:20	9
I Corinthians 16:13	11
2 Corinthians 3:18	12
Nehemiah 8:10	15
Matthew 25:21,23	15
Ephesians 6:11	20
Romans 1:15	25
2 Corinthians 12:9	26
Matthew 6:33	27
Hosea 10:12	29
I Chronicles 16:22	30
Matthew 16:23	32
Matthew 16:26	33
Malachi 3:8,10	34
Ruth 2:4	35

Biblical References Indexed Alpha-Numerical Order

Reference	Page
1 Peter 5:7	7
2 Corinthians 12:9	26
2 Corinthians 3:18	12
Ephesians 5:20	9
Ephesians 6:11	20
Hosea 10:12	29
I Chronicles 16:22	30
I Corinthians 16:13	11
Malachi 3:8,10	34
Mark 4:39	6
Matthew 16:23	32
Matthew 16:26	33
Matthew 25:21,23	15
Matthew 6:33	27
Nehemiah 8:10	15
Romans 1:15	25
Ruth 2:4	35

Made in the USA
Columbia, SC
06 March 2021